hebrews

the epistle of paul the apostle to the

hebrews

authorised king james version

printed by authority

published by canongate

with an introduction by | karen armstrong

First published in Great Britain in 1999
by Canongate Books Ltd
14 High Street, Edinburgh EH1 1TE

10 9 8 7 6 5 4 3 2 1

British Library Cataloguing-in-Publication Data
A catalogue record is available on request from
the British Library

ISBN 0 86241 974 3

Typeset by Palimpsest Book Production
Book design by Paddy Cramsie at et al
Printed and bound in Great Britain
by Caledonian International, Bishopbriggs

a note about pocket canons

The Authorised King James Version of the Bible, translated between 1603–11, coincided with an extraordinary flowering of English literature. This version, more than any other, and possibly more than any other work in history, has had an influence in shaping the language we speak and write today.

Twenty-four of the eighty original books of the King James Bible are brought to you in this series. They encompass categories as diverse as history, philosophy, law, poetry and fiction. Each Pocket Canon also has its own introduction, specially commissioned from an impressive range of writers, to provide a personal interpretation of the text and explore its contemporary relevance.

introduction by karen armstrong

Karen Armstrong's first book, the best-selling Through the Narrow Gate *(1981), described her seven years as a nun in a Roman Catholic order. She has published numerous books –* A History of God, *which has been translated into thirty languages,* A History of Jerusalem *and* In the Beginning: A New Reading of Genesis.

We are currently living in a time of religious transition. In many of the countries of Western Europe, atheism is on the increase, and the churches are emptying, being converted into art galleries, restaurants and warehouses. Even in the United States, where over ninety per cent of the population claim to believe in God, people are seeking new ways of thinking about religion and practising their faith. In our dramatically altered circumstances, the old symbols that once introduced people to a sacred dimension of existence no longer function so effectively. In the Christian world, some people are either abandoning the old forms, or trying to reinterpret such doctrines as the incarnation or the atonement in a way that makes sense to them at the beginning of the third Christian millennium.

The author of *The Epistle to the Hebrews* was writing at

another pivotal moment in religious history, when the traditional symbols of the divine in Judaism – the Law of Moses, the Jerusalem Temple, and the old covenant between God and the people of Israel – seemed increasingly unsatisfactory to a significant number of Jews who were also struggling to find new ways of being religious. During the first century CE, there were a number of different sects, which were attempting to reinterpret Judaism. The most popular of these sects was that of the Pharisees, who based their spirituality on the Law; they were the most progressive and innovative Jews of the period and wanted to bring the Law up to date, by amending the Law as found in scripture by developing an oral or customal law, based on the actual practice of Jews. They enjoyed the support of most of the ordinary people. The Saducees were mostly members of the aristocratic and priestly classes; they were traditionalists, who wanted to stick to the letter of the Law as found in the Bible; their piety centred on the ancient cult in the Temple. The Essenes were more radical; they believed that the End of Days was nigh and that the Judaism of their day was corrupt, and had withdrawn from mainstream society to await the final battle between the powers of good and evil; some had retreated to Qumran beside the Dead Sea, and lived in a quasi-monastic community.

Christianity began as yet another of these Jewish sects. Until St Paul took the new faith to the gentile world, the original disciples of Jesus had no intention of founding a new religion. They believed that Jesus had been the Messiah and that he would shortly return in glory to inaugurate

God's kingdom. They observed the Law and worshipped daily in the Temple, were regarded as devout and legitimate Jews, and were not eager to admit gentiles into their sect. The author of *Hebrews* was writing to a group of these Jewish Christians, but he was trying to persuade them to be more radical. He was almost certainly not St Paul, but was probably Paul's contemporary, writing during the 60s, some thirty years after Jesus's death. The Temple, whose rites he describes in such detail and which was destroyed by the Romans in 70 CE, was obviously still standing, but our author, like other Jews at this time, no longer felt that its rites and imagery yielded access to God. He and the Jewish Christians to whom he was writing were in a stage of transition; they were trying to decide what Jesus had meant to them and what his function was in their religious life. The recipients of his letter had various theories, but their roots were still in Judaism, whereas our author was beginning to break away from the traditional Jewish faith, and develop something new.

Our author is aware that he is being controversial, and that many of his readers still felt comfortable with the Temple liturgy. But he was not alone in discovering that these ancient rites, which had been profoundly satisfying to Jews for centuries and which had been crucial to their spiritual life, no longer spoke to him of God. The Qumran sect would have nothing whatever to do with the Temple; they believed that their community constituted a spiritual Temple and that when the Messiah returned at the End of Days, he would build a new Temple, not made by human hands but built miraculously by God himself. They denounced the Jerusalem priests as wicked and sinful, and looked forward to the arrival of a Messiah who would be a perfect priest of the House of Aaron. They clearly felt so uncomfortable with the Temple liturgy that they condemned it as perverse. The Pharisees were less extreme. They continued to worship in the Temple, but were also beginning to teach that charity and acts of loving kindness were just as effective a means of expiating sin as the old animal sacrifices. The loss of the Temple in 70 CE was a devastating blow, but Jews had already begun to retreat from it, and were thus able to make the transition to rabbinic Judaism with the minimum of fuss, encountering the divine presence in the sacred text of the Law rather than in a sacred building.

The author of *Hebrews*, like other Jewish Christians, shared many of the concerns of the Pharisees and the Essenes; like them, he was trying to find a new way to be Jewish, which put Jesus, the Messiah, at the centre of the picture instead of the Law and the Temple. The Temple liturgy seems to have died on him, and now left him cold. He was especially perturbed by the fact that the Jewish priests had to offer 'those sacrifices' 'continually', over and over again, 'year by year', and all to no avail, for these rituals 'can never take away sins' (10:1,11). He felt the same kind of frustration with the Temple as St Paul experienced about the Law, which, far from liberating Paul from his sins, had only made him more conscious of his sinfulness (*Romans* 7). Where the Pharisees and the Essenes found God in the Law and the sacred community, respectively, these Jewish Christians were making Jesus a symbol which brought them into the divine presence.

We should not underestimate the magnitude of this change. In almost every civilization in the ancient world, the Temple was one of the chief symbols of the divine. Indeed, religion was inconceivable without temple worship and animal sacrifice. When those Jews who had been deported to Babylon by Nebuchadnezzar in 586 BCE, when their Temple had been destroyed for the first time, asked how they could sing the Lord's song in an alien land (Psalm 137:4), they were not simply being maudlin or nostalgic about their ruined Temple on Mount Zion in Jerusalem. They were voicing a real theological difficulty. A deity was inaccessible to his worshippers if he did not have a shrine. Whereas today people feel they can encounter God and pray to him wherever they happen to be (in a field or a mountain-top, as well as a church), this was not so in the ancient world. A god could only meet his devotees in a place that he had chosen. The Temple was a replica of his home in the divine world, which mysteriously made him present here below. In premodern religion, the reproduction contained something of the original archetype and a symbol was inseparable from the spiritual entity to which it pointed. The effect of this was similar to the way the son of a dead friend brings the father into the room with him, because he reminds us physically of the deceased, and, at the same time, makes us feel his absence more acutely. The author of *Hebrews* takes this symbolic spirituality for granted; it is fundamental to his argument. The Jerusalem Temple, he explains, is a copy of God's spiritual Temple in the Heavenly Jerusalem; its rituals imitate the celestial liturgy in the Heavenly Sanctuary, and this process of *imitatio dei* (on which all premodern religion was based) brought something of that transcendent reality down to the world of men and women.

Our author understood the Temple symbolism, but, like other Jews, found that it no longer worked for him. The Temple and its cult seemed to him repetitious and pointless; these rites no longer yielded any sense of the divine. There are clear indications that Jews were not alone in this. In some parts of the Greek world, people were beginning to find Temple worship meaningless too, and had started to locate the divine in other symbols which did give them that sense of transcendance and ecstasy that human beings seem to need. Today those who do not find this enhanced life in religion, seek transcendence in art, music, literature, sport, or even in drugs. This shift from temple worship in late antiquity represented a major religious change. It would once have been considered the height of blasphemy to deny that the Temple gave men and women access to the divine, so essential had it been to the religious experience of humanity.

The Temple was an attempt to express an ineffable divine reality in human terms. Our doctrines (such as the Trinity, the Incarnation, the Atonement, or even the concept of a personal God) are also symbols, which attempt to give shape to our experience of the sacred. These doctrines cannot fully contain the reality of what we call 'God', any more than a building could. They can only point to a Reality which must surpass them, as it goes beyond all human categories and systems. Western Christians have tended to lose sight of the crucial fact that we can only speak of the divine in terms of signs and symbols. Since the scientific revolution of the sixteenth and seventeenth centuries, Western people have often assumed that 'God' was an objective but unseen reality (like the atom), and that our doctrines were accurate descriptions of this divine Fact. But theology should be regarded as poetry (Greek and Russian Orthodox Christians have always been aware of this). Theology is merely an attempt to express the inexpressible as felicitously as possible. But, as we all know, some of our poetic symbols lose their power and immediacy, as our circumstances change. Today many Christians feel that the ideas of a personal God or of the divinity of Jesus are absolutely essential to faith, but in the ancient world people felt just as strongly about the divine presence in the Temple. When a particular image of the sacred loses its valency, it does not mean that religion itself must die. The old symbol is often taken up and given fresh life in a new and different system.

That is what is happening in *The Epistle to the Hebrews*. Where once Temple worship gave all believers a direct experience of the numinous, our author clearly finds that the Temple is *only* a symbol. When the Prophet Isaiah had been able to see the divine presence and the heavenly sanctuary while he was worshipping in the Temple, seeing *through* the symbolism and the liturgy to the Reality behind it (*Isaiah* 6:1–4), our author can see no further than the physical rites. For him, they are simply rules about the outward life, and have no power to transform us interiorly; the Temple priests are obviously imperfect, since they are only human; the sacrifice of bulls and goats is messy and pointless; and the building itself clearly man-made. He can no longer see what Isaiah saw. In order to work effectively, a symbol has to be experienced as a direct link to the more elusive and transcendent reality to which it directs our attention, but our author can only see the Temple as a human artefact. Similarly, for many sceptics today, the conventional doctrines of Christianity, which for centuries gave people an immediate sense of God, seem nothing more than human constructs.

But instead of jettisoning the old symbol of the Temple, as the Qumran sect did, our author reinterprets it. He makes Christ the new High Priest. In the old cult, the High Priest entered the Holy of Holies (the innermost sanctum of the Temple, which re-presented [*sic*] the divine presence) once a year on the Day of Atonement. He alone could enter this most sacred place, and the people came into God's presence vicariously through this symbolic rite. The Holy of Holies was carefully designed to re-present God's Throne in the Heavenly Jerusalem. Now, by virtue of his sacrificial death, Christ had entered into the celestial sanctuary once and for all. He had bypassed the symbolism and introduced believers to the sacred Reality itself. For our author, the figure of Christ had become *the* new symbol that brought humanity to the divine; he was 'the express image of [God's] person' (1:3). (The Jerusalem Bible has been truer to the author's intention and to the old symbolic spirituality by rendering this 'a perfect copy of [God's] nature'). As a 'copy' of God in human form, Jesus gave our author a direct experience of the divine: when he contemplated the human figure of Jesus, he had a clear sense of what God was like. People had no further need of earthly symbols, therefore, since they had already gone directly into the divine presence with Christ; they had already passed over, in the person of their High Priest, into the next world:

> But ye are come unto mount Sion, and unto
> the city of the living God, the heavenly
> Jerusalem, and to an innumerable company
> of angels, to the general assembly and church
> of the firstborn, which are written in heaven,
> and to God, the Judge of all … (12:22–3)

Again, the Jerusalem Bible has preserved the original more forcefully than the King James version, by translating this last sentence: 'You have come to God himself.' In the person of their new High Priest, Christians have already come directly into the divine presence. They may feel that they are living a mundane life here below, but they are really with God in the Heavenly Jerusalem.

But, as with any religious symbolism, there were difficulties. Our author is poignantly aware that it is hard to live a religious life without any tangible replicas of the divine here below. Jesus had gone away, into another dimension, and Christians had to have faith in what was unseen. Their lives, as the author makes clear, were hard and full of suffering; how could they believe that they were already in Heaven? The epistle also makes it clear that the figure of

Christ was by no means firmly established as the only symbol that gave Christians a sense of God. Some of the recipients of his letter thought that angels were more effective mediators than Jesus; others were still drawn to the figure of Moses and the Law. This reminds us that Christianity did not spring forth ready-made from the minds of the apostles after the Resurrection. Christians had to work hard to make Jesus a viable symbol of the divine, using all their creative expertise. They would continue to discuss who and what Jesus had been and what he had meant to them for centuries. Western Christians would finally accept the ruling of the Council of Chalcedon (451) that Jesus had both a divine and a human nature, something that neither Paul nor the author of *Hebrews* (who saw Jesus only as a human 'copy' of God) had claimed. The Greek Orthodox Christians were not satisfied with Chalcedon and went on discussing Christology for another two hundred years. They developed quite a different notion of Jesus. Maximus the Confessor (*c.* 580–662), the founder of Byzantine theology, believed that God would have become human even if Adam had not sinned; Jesus had not died to atone for our sins, but he was the first human being to be wholly deified; what he had been, all Christians could be.

The point is that people who call themselves Christians have had very different ideas about God and Jesus over the years. Our theology has changed dramatically in the past, and can do so again. Today the old conciliar definitions about God or Jesus do not always speak to Christians or would-be Christians. They seem to belong to another age, and can appear to be as fabricated and arbitrary to many people as the old Temple and its liturgy had become for our author. *The Epistle to the Hebrews* reminds us that there is no need to repine if a rite, an image, or a doctrine dies on us. We can, like our author, use our imaginations to build on the past and create a symbol that will speak to us more eloquently and directly of the sacred.

the epistle of paul the apostle to the hebrews

God, who at sundry times and in divers manners spake in time past unto the fathers by the prophets, ²hath in these last days spoken unto us by his Son, whom he hath appointed heir of all things, by whom also he made the worlds, ³who being the brightness of his glory, and the express image of his person, and upholding all things by the word of his power, when he had by himself purged our sins, sat down on the right hand of the Majesty on high, ⁴being made so much better than the angles, as he hath by inheritance obtained a more excellent name than they.

⁵For unto which of the angels said he at any time, 'Thou art my Son, this day have I begotten thee?' And again, 'I will be to him a Father, and he shall be to me a Son?' ⁶And again, when he bringeth in the firstbegotten into the world, he saith, 'And let all the angels of God worship him.' ⁷And of the angels he saith, 'Who maketh his angels spirits, and his ministers a flame of fire.' ⁸But unto the Son he saith, 'Thy throne, O God, is for ever and ever: a sceptre of righteousness is the sceptre of thy kingdom. ⁹Thou hast loved righteousness, and hated iniquity; therefore God, even thy God, hath anointed thee with the oil of gladness above thy fellows.' ¹⁰And, 'Thou, Lord, in the beginning hast laid the foundation of the earth;

and the heavens are the works of thine hands: ¹¹ they shall perish, but thou remainest; and they all shall wax old as doth a garment; ¹² and as a vesture shalt thou fold them up, and they shall be changed; but thou art the same, and thy years shall not fail.' ¹³ But to which of the angels said he at any time, 'Sit on my right hand, until I make thine enemies thy footstool?' ¹⁴ Are they not all ministering spirits, sent forth to minister for them who shall be heirs of salvation?

2 Therefore we ought to give the more earnest heed to the things which we have heard, lest at any time we should let them slip. ² For if the word spoken by angels was stedfast, and every transgression and disobedience received a just recompence of reward, ³ how shall we escape, if we neglect so great salvation; which at the first began to be spoken by the Lord, and was confirmed unto us by them that heard him; ⁴ God also bearing them witness, both with signs and wonders, and with divers miracles, and gifts of the Holy Ghost, according to his own will?

⁵ For unto the angels hath he not put in subjection the world to come, whereof we speak. ⁶ But one in a certain place testified, saying, 'What is man, that thou art mindful of him? Or the son of man, that thou visitest him? ⁷ Thou madest him a little lower than the angels; thou crownedst him with glory and honour, and didst set him over the works of thy hands: ⁸ thou hast put all things in subjection under his feet.' For in that he put all in subjection under him, he left nothing that is not put under him. But now we see not yet all things put under him. ⁹ But we see Jesus, who was made a little lower than the angels for the suffering of death, crowned with glory and honour; that he by the grace of God should taste death for every man.

¹⁰ For it became him, for whom are all things, and by whom are all things, in bringing many sons unto glory, to make the captain of their salvation perfect through sufferings. ¹¹ For both he that sanctifieth and they who are sanctified are all of one, for which cause he is not ashamed to call

them brethren, [12] saying, 'I will declare thy name unto my brethren, in the midst of the church will I sing praise unto thee.' [13] And again, 'I will put my trust in him.' And again, 'Behold I and the children which God hath given me.'

[14] Forasmuch then as the children are partakers of flesh and blood, he also himself likewise took part of the same; that through death he might destroy him that had the power of death, that is, the devil; [15] and deliver them who through fear of death were all their lifetime subject to bondage. [16] For verily he took not on him the nature of angels; but he took on him the seed of Abraham. [17] Wherefore in all things it behoved him to be made like unto his brethren, that he might be a merciful and faithful high priest in things pertaining to God, to make reconciliation for the sins of the people. [18] For in that he himself hath suffered being tempted, he is able to succour them that are tempted.

3 Wherefore, holy brethren, partakers of the heavenly calling, consider the Apostle and High Priest of our profession, Christ Jesus, ² who was faithful to him that appointed him, as also Moses was faithful in all his house. ³ For this man was counted worthy of more glory than Moses, inasmuch as he who hath builded the house hath more honour than the house. ⁴ For every house is builded by some man; but he that built all things is God. ⁵ And Moses verily was faithful in all his house, as a servant, for a testimony of those things which were to be spoken after; ⁶ but Christ as a son over his own house; whose house are we, if we hold fast the confidence and the rejoicing of the hope firm unto the end.

⁷ Wherefore (as the Holy Ghost saith) 'To day if ye will hear his voice, ⁸ harden not your hearts, as in the provocation, in the day of temptation in the wilderness: ⁹ when your fathers tempted me, proved me, and saw my works forty years. ¹⁰ Wherefore I was grieved with that generation, and said, "They do alway err in their heart; and they have not known my ways." ¹¹ So I sware in my wrath, "They shall not enter into my rest."' ¹² Take heed, brethren, lest there be in any of you an evil heart of unbelief, in departing from the living God. ¹³ But exhort one another daily, while it is called 'To day'; lest any of you be hardened through the deceitfulness of sin. ¹⁴ For we are made partakers of Christ, if we hold the beginning of our confidence stedfast unto the end, ¹⁵ while it is said, 'To day if ye will hear his voice, harden not your hearts, as in the provocation.' ¹⁶ For some, when they

had heard, did provoke: howbeit not all that came out of Egypt by Moses. ¹⁷ But with whom was he grieved forty years? Was it not with them that had sinned, whose carcases fell in the wilderness? ¹⁸ And to whom sware he that they should not enter into his rest, but to them that believed not? ¹⁹ So we see that they could not enter in because of unbelief.

4 Let us therefore fear, lest, a promise being left us of entering into his rest, any of you should seem to come short of it. ² For unto us was the gospel preached, as well as unto them; but the word preached did not profit them, not being mixed with faith in them that heard it. ³ For we which have believed to enter into rest, as he said, 'As I have sworn in my wrath, if they shall enter into my rest': although the works were finished from the foundation of the world. ⁴ For he spake in a certain place of the seventh day on this wise, 'And God did rest the seventh day from all his works.' ⁵ And in this place again, 'If they shall enter into my rest.' ⁶ Seeing therefore it remaineth that some must enter therein, and they to whom it was first preached entered not in because of unbelief: ⁷ again, he limiteth a certain day, saying in David, 'To day', after so long a time; as it is said, 'To day if ye will hear his voice, harden not your hearts.' ⁸ For if Jesus had given them rest, then would he not afterward have spoken of another day. ⁹ There remaineth therefore a rest to the people of God. ¹⁰ For he that is entered into his rest, he also hath ceased from his own works, as God did from his. ¹¹ Let us labour therefore to enter into that rest, lest any man fall after the same example of unbelief.

¹² For the word of God is quick, and powerful, and sharper than any two-edged sword, piercing even to the dividing asunder of soul and spirit, and of the joints and marrow, and is a discerner of the thoughts and intents of the heart. ¹³ Neither is there any creature that is not manifest in his sight; but all things are naked and opened unto the eyes

of him with whom we have to do.

¹⁴ Seeing then that we have a great high priest, that is passed into the heavens, Jesus the Son of God, let us hold fast our profession. ¹⁵ For we have not an high priest which cannot be touched with the feeling of our infirmities; but was in all points tempted like as we are, yet without sin. ¹⁶ Let us therefore come boldly unto the throne of grace, that we may obtain mercy, and find grace to help in time of need.

5 For every high priest taken from among men is ordained for men in things pertaining to God, that he may offer both gifts and sacrifices for sins, ² who can have compassion on the ignorant, and on them that are out of the way; for that he himself also is compassed with infirmity. ³And by reason hereof he ought, as for the people, so also for himself, to offer for sins. ⁴And no man taketh this honour unto himself, but he that is called of God, as was Aaron.

⁵ So also Christ glorified not himself to be made an high priest; but he that said unto him, 'Thou art my Son, to day have I begotten thee.' ⁶As he saith also in another place, 'Thou art a priest for ever after the order of Melchisedec.'

⁷ Who in the days of his flesh, when he had offered up prayers and supplications with strong crying and tears unto him that was able to save him from death, and was heard in that he feared; ⁸ though he were a Son, yet learned he obedience by the things which he suffered; ⁹and being made perfect, he became the author of eternal salvation unto all them that obey him; ¹⁰called of God an high priest after the order of Melchisedec.

¹¹Of whom we have many things to say, and hard to be uttered, seeing ye are dull of hearing. ¹²For when for the time ye ought to be teachers, ye have need that one teach you again which be the first principles of the oracles of God; and are become such as have need of milk, and not of strong meat. ¹³For every one that useth milk is unskilful in the word of righeousness: for he is a babe. ¹⁴But strong meat belongeth to them that are of full age, even those who by reason of use have their senses exercised to discern both good and evil.

6 Therefore leaving the principles of the doctrine of Christ, let us go on unto perfection; not laying again the foundation of repentance from dead works, and of faith toward God, ² of the doctrine of baptisms, and of laying on of hands, and of resurrection of the dead, and of eternal judgment. ³ And this will we do, if God permit. ⁴ For it is impossible for those who were once enlightened, and have tasted of the heavenly gift, and were made partakers of the Holy Ghost, ⁵ and have tasted the good word of God, and the powers of the world to come, ⁶ if they shall fall away, to renew them again unto repentance; seeing they crucify to themselves the Son of God afresh, and put him to an open shame. ⁷ For the earth which drinketh in the rain that cometh oft upon it, and bringeth forth herbs meet for them by whom it is dressed, receiveth blessing from God. ⁸ But that which beareth thorns and briers is rejected, and is nigh unto cursing; whose end is to be burned.

⁹ But, beloved, we are persuaded better things of you, and things that accompany salvation, though we thus speak. ¹⁰ For God is not unrighteous to forget your work and labour of love, which ye have shewed toward his name, in that ye have ministered to the saints, and do minister. ¹¹ And we desire that every one of you do shew the same diligence to the full assurance of hope unto the end, ¹² that ye be not slothful, but followers of them who through faith and patience inherit the promises.

¹³ For when God made promise to Abraham, because he could swear by no greater, he sware by himself, ¹⁴ saying,

'Surely blessing I will bless thee, and multiplying I will multiply thee.' ¹⁵And so, after he had patiently endured, he obtained the promise. ¹⁶For men verily swear by the greater, and an oath for confirmation is to them an end of all strife. ¹⁷Wherein God, willing more abundantly to shew unto the heirs of promise the immutability of his counsel, confirmed it by an oath: ¹⁸that by two immutable things, in which it was impossible for God to lie, we might have a strong consolation, who have fled for refuge to lay hold upon the hope set before us, ¹⁹which hope we have as an anchor of the soul, both sure and stedfast, and which entereth into that within the veil; ²⁰whither the forerunner is for us entered, even Jesus, made an high priest for ever after the order of Melchisedec.

7 For this Melchisedec, king of Salem, priest of the most high God, who met Abraham returning from the slaughter of the kings, and blessed him, ²to whom also Abraham gave a tenth part of all; first being by interpretation King of righteousness, and after that also King of Salem, which is, King of peace; ³without father, without mother, without descent, having neither beginning of days, nor end of life; but made like unto the Son of God; abideth a priest continually.

⁴Now consider how great this man was, unto whom even the patriarch Abraham gave the tenth of the spoils. ⁵And verily they that are of the sons of Levi, who receive the office of the priesthood, have a commandment to take tithes of the people according to the law, that is, of their brethren, though they come out of the loins of Abraham, ⁶but he whose descent is not counted from them received tithes of Abraham, and blessed him that had the promises. ⁷And without all contradiction the less is blessed of the better. ⁸And here men that die receive tithes; but there he receiveth them, of whom it is witnessed that he liveth. ⁹And as I may so say, Levi also, who receiveth tithes, payed tithes in Abraham. ¹⁰For he was yet in the loins of his father, when Melchisedec met him.

¹¹If therefore perfection were by the Levitical priesthood (for under it the people received the law), what further need was there that another priest should rise after the order of Melchisedec, and not be called after the order of Aaron? ¹²For the priesthood being changed, there is made of necessity a change also of the law. ¹³For he of whom these things are spoken pertaineth to another tribe, of which no man gave attendance at the altar. ¹⁴For it is evident that our Lord sprang out of Juda;

of which tribe Moses spake nothing concerning priesthood.

¹⁵And it is yet far more evident, for that after the similitude of Melchisedec there ariseth another priest, ¹⁶who is made, not after the law of a carnal commandment, but after the power of an endless life. ¹⁷For he testifieth, 'Thou art a priest for ever after the order of Melchisedec.' ¹⁸For there is verily a disannulling of the commandment going before for the weakness and unprofitableness thereof. ¹⁹For the law made nothing perfect, but the bringing in of a better hope did; by the which we draw nigh unto God. ²⁰And inasmuch as not without an oath he was made priest ²¹(for those priests were made without an oath; but this with an oath by him that said unto him, 'The Lord sware and will not repent, Thou art a priest for ever after the order of Melchisedec'). ²²By so much was Jesus made a surety of a better testament.

²³And they truly were many priests, because they were not suffered to continue by reason of death: ²⁴But this man, because he continueth ever, hath an unchangeable priesthood. ²⁵Wherefore he is able also to save them to the uttermost that come unto God by him, seeing he ever liveth to make intercession for them.

²⁶For such an high priest became us, who is holy, harmless, undefiled, separate from sinners, and made higher than the heavens; ²⁷who needeth not daily, as those high priests, to offer up sacrifice, first for his own sins, and then for the people's, for this he did once, when he offered up himself. ²⁸For the law maketh men high priests which have infirmity; but the word of the oath, which was since the law, maketh the Son, who is consecrated for evermore.

8 Now of the things which we have spoken this is the sum: we have such an high priest, who is set on the right hand of the throne of the Majesty in the heavens; [2] a minister of the sanctuary, and of the true tabernacle, which the Lord pitched, and not man. [3] For every high priest is ordained to offer gifts and sacrifices: wherefore it is of necessity that this man have somewhat also to offer. [4] For if he were on earth, he should not be a priest, seeing that there are priests that offer gifts according to the law, [5] who serve unto the example and shadow of heavenly things, as Moses was admonished of God when he was about to make the tabernacle, for, 'See,' saith he, 'that thou make all things according to the pattern shewed to thee in the mount.' [6] But now hath he obtained a more excellent ministry, by how much also he is the mediator of a better covenant, which was established upon better promises. [7] For if that first convenant had been faultless, then should no place have been sought for the second.

[8] For finding fault with them, he saith, 'Behold, the days come,' saith the Lord, 'when I will make a new covenant with the house of Israel and with the house of Judah: [9] not according to the covenant that I made with their fathers in the day when I took them by the hand to lead them out of the land of Egypt; because they continued not in my covenant, and I regarded them not,' saith the Lord. [10] 'For this is the covenant that I will make with the house of Israel after those days,' saith the Lord; 'I will put my laws into their mind, and write them in their hearts: and I will be to

them a God, and they shall be to me a people: "and they shall not teach every man his neighbour, and every man his brother, saying, "Know the Lord," for all shall know me, from the least to the greatest. ¹²For I will be merciful to their unrighteousness, and their sins and their iniquities will I remember no more.' ¹³In that he saith, 'A new covenant', he hath made the first old. Now that which decayeth and waxeth old is ready to vanish away.

9 Then verily the first covenant had also ordinances of divine service, and a worldly sanctuary. ² For there was a tabernacle made; the first, wherein was the candlestick, and the table, and the shewbread; which is called the sanctuary. ³And after the second veil, the tabernacle which is called the Holiest of all, ⁴ which had the golden censer, and the ark of the covenant overlaid round about with gold, wherein was the golden pot that had manna, and Aaron's rod that budded, and the tables of the covenant; ⁵and over it the cherubims of glory shadowing the mercyseat; of which we cannot now speak particularly.

⁶ Now when these things were thus ordained, the priests went always into the first tabernacle, accomplishing the service of God. ⁷ But into the second went the high priest alone once every year, not without blood, which he offered for himself, and for the errors of the people: ⁸ the Holy Ghost this signifying, that the way into the holiest of all was not yet made manifest, while as the first tabernacle was yet standing, ⁹ which was a figure for the time then present, in which were offered both gifts and sacrifices, that could not make him that did the service perfect, as pertaining to the conscience, ¹⁰ which stood only in meats and drinks, and divers washings, and carnal ordinances, imposed on them until the time of reformation.

¹¹ But Christ being come an high priest of good things to come, by a greater and more perfect tabernacle, not made with hands, that is to say, not of this building; ¹² neither by the blood of goats and calves, but by his own blood he

16

entered in once into the holy place, having obtained eternal redemption for us. ¹³ For if the blood of bulls and of goats, and the ashes of an heifer sprinkling the unclean, sanctifieth to the purifying of the flesh: ¹⁴ how much more shall the blood of Christ, who through the eternal Spirit offered himself without spot to God, purge your conscience from dead works to serve the living God?

¹⁵ And for this cause he is the mediator of the new testament, that by means of death, for the redemption of the transgressions that were under the first testament, they which are called might receive the promise of eternal inheritance. ¹⁶ For where a testament is, there must also of necessity be the death of the testator. ¹⁷ For a testament is of force after men are dead: otherwise it is of no strength at all while the testator liveth. ¹⁸ Whereupon neither the first testament was dedicated without blood. ¹⁹ For when Moses had spoken every precept to all the people according to the law, he took the blood of calves and of goats, with water, and scarlet wool, and hyssop, and sprinkled both the book, and all the people, ²⁰ saying, 'This is the blood of the testament which God hath enjoined unto you.' ²¹ Moreover he sprinkled with blood both the tabernacle, and all the vessels of the ministry. ²² And almost all things are by the law purged with blood; and without shedding of blood is no remission.

²³ It was therefore necessary that the patterns of things in the heavens should be purified with these; but the heavenly things themselves with better sacrifices than these. ²⁴ For Christ is not entered into the holy places made with hands,

which are the figures of the true; but into heaven itself, now to appear in the presence of God for us, [25] nor yet that he should offer himself often, as the high priest entereth into the holy place every year with blood of others, [26] for then must he often have suffered since the foundation of the world; but now once in the end of the world hath he appeared to put away sin by the sacrifice of himself. [27] And as it is appointed unto men once to die, but after this the judgment: [28] so Christ was once offered to bear the sins of many; and unto them that look for him shall he appear the second time without sin unto salvation.

10 For the law having a shadow of good things to come, and not the very image of the things, can never with those sacrifices which they offered year by year continually make the comers thereunto perfect. ² For then would they not have ceased to be offered? Because that the worshippers once purged should have had no more conscience of sins. ³ But in those sacrifices there is a remembrance again made of sins every year. ⁴ For it is not possible that the blood of bulls and of goats should take away sins. ⁵ Wherefore when he cometh into the world, he saith, 'Sacrifice and offering thou wouldest not, but a body hast thou prepared me: ⁶ in burnt offerings and sacrifices for sin thou hast had no pleasure.' ⁷ Then said I, 'Lo, I come (in the volume of the book it is written of me), to do thy will, O God.' ⁸ Above when he said, 'Sacrifice and offering and burnt offerings and offering for sin thou wouldest not, neither hadst pleasure therein; which are offered by the law'; ⁹ then said he, 'Lo, I come to do thy will, O God.' He taketh away the first, that he may establish the second. ¹⁰ By the which will we are sanctified through the offering of the body of Jesus Christ once for all.

¹¹ And every priest standeth daily ministering and offering oftentimes the same sacrifices, which can never take away sins; ¹² but this man, after he had offered one sacrifice for sins for ever, sat down on the right hand of God; ¹³ from henceforth expecting till his enemies be made his footstool. ¹⁴ For by one offering he hath perfected for ever them that are sanctified. ¹⁵ Whereof the Holy Ghost also is a witness to us, for after that he had said before, ¹⁶ 'This is the covenant that I

will make with them after those days,' saith the Lord, 'I will put my laws into their hearts, and in their minds will I write them; ¹⁷and their sins and iniquities will I remember no more.' ¹⁸Now where remission of these is, there is no more offering for sin.

¹⁹Having therefore, brethren, boldness to enter into the holiest by the blood of Jesus, ²⁰by a new and living way, which he hath consecrated for us, through the veil, that is to say, his flesh; ²¹and having an high priest over the house of God; ²²let us draw near with a true heart in full assurance of faith, having our hearts sprinkled from an evil conscience, and our bodies washed with pure water ²³Let us hold fast the profession of our faith without wavering (for he is faithful that promised); ²⁴and let us consider one another to provoke unto love and to good works: ²⁵not forsaking the assembling of ourselves together, as the manner of some is; but exhorting one another; and so much the more, as ye see the day approaching.

²⁶For if we sin wilfully after that we have received the knowledge of the truth, there remaineth no more sacrifice for sins, ²⁷but a certain fearful looking for of judgment and fiery indignation, which shall devour the adversaries. ²⁸He that despised Moses' law died without mercy under two or three witnesses: ²⁹of how much sorer punishment, suppose ye, shall he be thought worthy, who hath trodden under foot the Son of God, and hath counted the blood of the covenant, wherewith he was sanctified, an unholy thing, and hath done despite unto the Spirit of grace? ³⁰For we know him

that hath said, 'Vengeance belongeth unto me, I will recompense,' saith the Lord. And again, 'The Lord shall judge his people.' [31] It is a fearful thing to fall into the hands of the living God.

[32] But call to remembrance the former days, in which, after ye were illuminated, ye endured a great fight of afflictions; [33] partly, whilst ye were made a gazing-stock both by reproaches and afflictions; and partly, whilst ye became companions of them that were so used. [34] For ye had compassion of me in my bonds, and took joyfully the spoiling of your goods, knowing in yourselves that ye have in heaven a better and an enduring substance. [35] Cast not away therefore your confidence, which hath great recompence of reward. [36] For ye have need of patience, that, after ye have done the will of God, ye might receive the promise. [37] For yet a little while, and he that shall come will come, and will not tarry. [38] Now the just shall live by faith; but if any man draw back, my soul shall have no pleasure in him. [39] But we are not of them who draw back unto perdition; but of them that believe to the saving of the soul.

11 Now faith is the substance of things hoped for, the evidence of things not seen. ²For by it the elders obtained a good report. ³Through faith we understand that the worlds were framed by the word of God, so that things which are seen were not made of things which do appear.

⁴By faith Abel offered unto God a more excellent sacrifice than Cain, by which he obtained witness that he was righteous, God testifying of his gifts: and by it he being dead yet speaketh. ⁵By faith Enoch was translated that he should not see death; and was not found, because God had translated him, for before his translation he had this testimony, that he pleased God. ⁶But without faith it is impossible to please him, for he that cometh to God must believe that he is, and that he is a rewarder of them that diligently seek him. ⁷By faith Noah, being warned of God of things not seen as yet, moved with fear, prepared an ark to the saving of his house; by the which he condemned the world, and became heir of the righteousness which is by faith.

⁸By faith Abraham, when he was called to go out into a place which he should after receive for an inheritance, obeyed; and he went out, not knowing whither he went. ⁹By faith he sojourned in the land of promise, as in a strange country, dwelling in tabernacles with Isaac and Jacob, the heirs with him of the same promise, ¹⁰for he looked for a city which hath foundations, whose builder and maker is God. ¹¹Through faith also Sara herself received strength to conceive seed, and was delivered of a child when she was past age, because she judged him faithful who had promised.

¹²Therefore sprang there even of one, and him as good as dead, so many as the stars of the sky in multitude, and as the sand which is by the sea shore innumerable.

¹³These all died in faith, not having received the promises, but having seen them afar off, and were persuaded of them, and embraced them, and confessed that they were strangers and pilgrims on the earth. ¹⁴For they that say such things declare plainly that they seek a country. ¹⁵And truly, if they had been mindful of that country from whence they came out, they might have had opportunity to have returned. ¹⁶But now they desire a better country, that is, an heavenly: wherefore God is not ashamed to be called their God, for he hath prepared for them a city.

¹⁷By faith Abraham, when he was tried, offered up Isaac: and he that had received the promises offered up his only begotten son, ¹⁸of whom it was said, 'That in Isaac shall thy seed be called,' ¹⁹accounting that God was able to raise him up, even from the dead; from whence also he received him in a figure. ²⁰By faith Isaac blessed Jacob and Esau concerning things to come. ²¹By faith Jacob, when he was a dying, blessed both the sons of Joseph; and worshipped, leaning upon the top of his staff. ²²By faith Joseph, when he died, made mention of the departing of the children of Israel; and gave commandment concerning his bones.

²³By faith Moses, when he was born, was hid three months of his parents, because they saw he was a proper child; and they were not afraid of the king's commandment. ²⁴By faith Moses, when he was come to years, refused to be

called the son of Pharaoh's daughter; ²⁵choosing rather to suffer affliction with the people of God, than to enjoy the pleasures of sin for a season; ²⁶esteeming the reproach of Christ greater riches than the treasures in Egypt, for he had respect unto the recompence of the reward. ²⁷By faith he forsook Egypt, not fearing the wrath of the king, for he endured, as seeing him who is invisible. ²⁸Through faith he kept the passover, and the sprinkling of blood, lest he that destroyed the firstborn should touch them.

²⁹By faith they passed through the Red sea as by dry land, which the Egyptians assaying to do were drowned. ³⁰By faith the walls of Jericho fell down, after they were compassed about seven days. ³¹By faith the harlot Rahab perished not with them that believed not, when she had received the spies with peace.

³²And what shall I more say? For the time would fail me to tell of Gedeon, and of Barak, and of Samson, and of Jephthae; of David also, and Samuel, and of the prophets; ³³who through faith subdued kingdoms, wrought righteousness, obtained promises, stopped the mouths of lions, ³⁴quenched the violence of fire, escaped the edge of the sword, out of weakness were made strong, waxed valiant in fight, turned to flight the armies of the aliens. ³⁵Women received their dead raised to life again: and others were tortured, not accepting deliverance; that they might obtain a better resurrection: ³⁶and others had trial of cruel mockings and scourgings, yea, moreover of bonds and imprisonment: ³⁷they were stoned, they were sawn asunder, were tempted, were slain

with the sword: they wandered about in sheepskins and goatskins; being destitute, afflicted, tormented ³⁸(of whom the world was not worthy): they wandered in deserts, and in mountains, and in dens and caves of the earth.

³⁹And these all, having obtained a good report through faith, received not the promise, ⁴⁰ God having provided some better thing for us, that they without us should not be made perfect.

12 Wherefore seeing we also are compassed about with so great a cloud of witnesses, let us lay aside every weight, and the sin which doth so easily beset us, and let us run with patience the race that is set before us, ² looking unto Jesus the author and finisher of our faith; who for the joy that was set before him endured the cross, despising the shame, and is set down at the right hand of the throne of God.

³ For consider him that endured such contradiction of sinners against himself, lest ye be wearied and faint in your minds. ⁴ Ye have not yet resisted unto blood, striving against sin. ⁵ And ye have forgotten the exhortation which speaketh unto you as unto children, 'My son, despise not thou the chastening of the Lord, nor faint when thou art rebuked of him, ⁶ for whom the Lord loveth he chasteneth, and scourgeth every son whom he receiveth.' ⁷ If ye endure chastening, God dealeth with you as with sons; for what son is he whom the father chasteneth not? ⁸ But if ye be without chastisement, whereof all are partakers, then are ye bastards, and not sons. ⁹ Furthermore we have had fathers of our flesh which corrected us, and we gave them reverence: shall we not much rather be in subjection unto the Father of spirits, and live? ¹⁰ For they verily for a few days chastened us after their own pleasure; but he for our profit, that we might be partakers of his holiness. ¹¹ Now no chastening for the present seemeth to be joyous, but grievous: nevertheless afterward it yieldeth the peaceable fruit of righteousness unto them which are exercised thereby.

¹² Wherefore lift up the hands which hang down, and the feeble knees; ¹³ and make straight paths for your feet, lest that which is lame be turned out of the way; but let it rather be healed.

¹⁴ Follow peace with all men, and holiness, without which no man shall see the Lord: ¹⁵ looking diligently lest any man fail of the grace of God; lest any root of bitterness springing up trouble you, and thereby many be defiled; ¹⁶ lest there be any fornicator, or profane person, as Esau, who for one morsel of meat sold his birthright. ¹⁷ For ye know how that afterward, when he would have inherited the blessing, he was rejected, for he found no place of repentance, though he sought it carefully with tears.

¹⁸ For ye are not come unto the mount that might be touched, and that burned with fire, nor unto blackness, and darkness, and tempest, ¹⁹ and the sound of a trumpet, and the voice of words; which voice they that heard intreated that the word should not be spoken to them any more ²⁰(for they could not endure that which was commanded, 'And if so much as a beast touch the mountain, it shall be stoned, or thrust through with a dart': ²¹ and so terrible was the sight, that Moses said, 'I exceedingly fear and quake'): ²² but ye are come unto mount Sion, and unto the city of the living God, the heavenly Jerusalem, and to an innumerable company of angels, ²³ to the general assembly and church of the firstborn, which are written in heaven, and to God the Judge of all, and to the spirits of just men made perfect, ²⁴ and to Jesus the mediator of the new covenant, and to the blood of sprink-

ling, that speaketh better things than that of Abel.

²⁵ See that ye refuse not him that speaketh. For if they escaped not who refused him that spake on earth, much more shall not we escape, if we turn away from him that speaketh from heaven, ²⁶ whose voice then shook the earth: but now he hath promised, saying, 'Yet once more I shake not the earth only, but also heaven.' ²⁷And this word, 'Yet once more' signifieth the removing of those things that are shaken, as of things that are made, that those things which cannot be shaken may remain. ²⁸ Wherefore we receiving a kingdom which cannot be moved, let us have grace, whereby we may serve God acceptably with reverence and godly fear, ²⁹ for our God is a consuming fire.

13 Let brotherly love continue. ² Be not forgetful to entertain strangers, for thereby some have entertained angels unawares. ³ Remember them that are in bonds, as bound with them; and them which suffer adversity, as being yourselves also in the body. ⁴ Marriage is honourable in all, and the bed undefiled, but whoremongers and adulterers God will judge. ⁵ Let your conversation be without covetousness; and be content with such things as ye have, for he hath said, 'I will never leave thee, nor forsake thee.' ⁶ So that we may boldly say, 'The Lord is my helper, and I will not fear what man shall do unto me.'

⁷ Remember them which have the rule over you, who have spoken unto you the word of God, whose faith follow, considering the end of their conversation. ⁸ Jesus Christ the same yesterday, and to day, and for ever. ⁹ Be not carried about with divers and strange doctrines. For it is a good thing that the heart be established with grace; not with meats, which have not profited them that have been occupied therein. ¹⁰ We have an altar, whereof they have no right to eat which serve the tabernacle. ¹¹ For the bodies of those beasts, whose blood is brought into the sanctuary by the high priest for sin, are burned without the camp. ¹² Wherefore Jesus also, that he might sanctify the people with his own blood, suffered without the gate. ¹³ Let us go forth therefore unto him without the camp, bearing his reproach. ¹⁴ For here have we no continuing city, but we seek one to come. ¹⁵ By him therefore let us offer the sacrifice of praise to God continually, that is, the fruit of our lips giving thanks to his

name. ¹⁶But to do good and to communicate forget not, for with such sacrifices God is well pleased.

¹⁷Obey them that have the rule over you, and submit yourselves, for they watch for your souls, as they that must give account, that they may do it with joy, and not with grief, for that is unprofitable for you.

¹⁸Pray for us, for we trust we have a good conscience, in all things willing to live honestly. ¹⁹But I beseech you the rather to do this, that I may be restored to you the sooner.

²⁰Now the God of peace, that brought again from the dead our Lord Jesus, that great shepherd of the sheep, through the blood of the everlasting covenant, ²¹make you perfect in every good work to do his will, working in you that which is wellpleasing in his sight, through Jesus Christ; to whom be glory for ever and ever. Amen.

²²And I beseech you, brethren, suffer the word of exhortation, for I have written a letter unto you in few words. ²³Know ye that our brother Timothy is set at liberty; with whom, if he come shortly, I will see you. ²⁴Salute all them that have the rule over you, and all the saints. They of Italy salute you. ²⁵Grace be with you all. Amen.